EXTRAORDINARY MAGIC

The Storytelling Life of Virginia Hamilton

Poems and Pictures by
NINA CREWS

Christy Ottaviano Books
LITTLE, BROWN AND COMPANY
New York Boston

To my parents, Donald Crews and Ann Jonas Crews,
and to Susan Hirschman, editor and friend
to both Virginia and me

ABOUT THIS BOOK

The illustrations for this book were created digitally using Adobe Photoshop. This book was edited by Christy Ottaviano and designed by Tracy Shaw. The production was supervised by Nyamekye Waliyaya, and the production editor was Annie McDonnell. The text was set in Metropolis, and the display types are Benton Sans and Fairwater Solid Serif.

By the age of four or five,
we have experienced everything we need
to write fiction. . . .

—VIRGINIA HAMILTON

VIRGINIA

Etta Belle and
Kenneth Hamilton
named their last baby
Virginia. A pretty name for a girl
that is also the name of a place.

The birthplace of
Virginia's grandfather, Levi.
Born in slavery. His story—
history to be remembered,
but not repeated.

Virginia carried this
story in her name.
History that would inspire
the writer she grew up
to be.

FLY

Grandpa Levi's mother
was remembered
for her courage.
For her decision
to fly with her baby
to freedom.

Flying through
forests on fast feet.
Over mountains.
Across the Ohio River.
To a place where Levi
could grow up
free.

MOTHER

One spring morning,
Mother and Virginia were doing
chores in the quiet house.
Hanging laundry, making beds.

Suddenly the wind shook the house
with a loud howl and moan.
The world outside turned wild—
gray, purple, and green. So scary!

"Don't worry, Ginny," said Mother.
"See how Grandmother Lilac bows down.
And the trees bend with her.
Here comes the wind! *Whee!*"

Together they watched the storm—
gray, purple, and green.
It wasn't so scary now. Mother's words
had turned the wind into a dance.

Whee!

FREE

Young Virginia felt free.
Free standing in an open field
glittering in golden sunlight.
Free enjoying a soft breeze
on a warm summer day.

Free to visit Aunt Sarah and
Cousin Marlene down the road.
Virginia's walk ending with
a cool drink of water and
a welcoming hug.

Young Virginia felt free.
She was the last baby
in the family, and her mother and
father worried less. "She's fine,"
they said. "Just let Ginny be."

Virginia was free.
To be a dreamer.
To be a wanderer.
To be her own unique self.
Free to be.

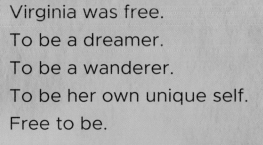

TIME

Dad's days began as the sky
brightened and birds awoke.
The rest of the family still in bed.

No time for himself. Not yet.
He had two jobs. Farm
chores at dawn. The day
spent serving food to
young scholars in the
Antioch dining hall.

His back straight,
shoulders square,
his head held high.

His time was later, in the yard
with Virginia as crickets chirped
their nighttime serenade.
His time to tell stories and
play his mandolin.

To share knowledge about
W. E. B. Du Bois, Ida B. Wells,
and Florence Mills. Black
people who made important
contributions to America's story.

Dad sat with his back straight,
shoulders square, his
head held high, and
played his mandolin.
Keeping time.

LIES

"Did it really happen like that?"

The grown-ups in Virginia's family
knew that a good story doesn't
have to be exactly true.
The storyteller might add
a bit of creativity. A joke. A wish.
A promise. Might make
the tale somewhat bigger than,
better than, real life.
Lies.

Did Virginia really believe that
Blind Martha walked that long,
dusty road all by herself?
Or that anyone, seeing or blind,
could find where a log cabin
stood in the woods years ago?
But wasn't it wonderful to
imagine that a person could
always find their way home?

STARS

Stars glittered in a coal-black sky,
high and far above. Nighttime in the country.
In the Hamilton house conversation buzzed.
Another universe with closer stars.

Buster had won a basketball trophy.
Nina just finished her first week at college.
Bill's stories always made them laugh.
Father played his mandolin beautifully.

Mother, father, sisters, brothers—
they were stars, every one!
Virginia's family shone brightly in her eyes.
Could she be a star, too?

DREAMS

Watch out for the Faceless One!
It chases Virginia in sleep.
Startles her awake with a cry.
Her big sisters hug her
close, but they can't stop
that scary dream from
coming back night
after night.

But then one night,
Virginia dreamed an idea.
When the Faceless One chased her,
she flapped her arms fast!
She rose up and up!
High into the sky and
flew toward the sun.

Glorious sun! Her fears
shivered in the bright light.
Magnificent sun! She has won!
Virginia's nightmare has vanished.

WRITER

Virginia had scared away
the Faceless One with her
imagination. What power!
She decided that she
would become
a writer.

Nine-year-old Virginia
told everyone about
her future career, her family
and her teachers at school.
Nobody laughed or said,
"You can't do that."

She began with "The Notebook."
Filled it with mysteries.
Page after page of family
drama—love, loss, and rage.
"What did it all mean?"
wondered the writer.

COUSINS

"This was my idea! I'm selling berries today!" Virginia fussed while Marlene filled her berry basket.

Cousins! Almost a sister or a brother. Sometimes a best friend and sometimes not. Virginia didn't want to share.

But she did it anyway. Two cousins. One fresh-picked berry business. Door-to-door sales to the ladies from the AME Church.

Two cousins who earned enough money
for a movie and popcorn. *Frankenstein*
or *Wolfman* at the Little Theater.

Two cousins who walked home as
darkness gathered in tall trees.
Cousins giggling, whispering.

Keeping lookout for movie monsters
lurking in the shadows.
Cousins.

HOGS

They snuffed and snorted and grunted.
The hogs wallowed in the mud outside the barn.
The scent of hay and manure filled the air.

She shushed and tsked and
told the hogs to be just a little bit quieter.
Didn't they know that she was writing her novel?

Virginia filled page after page of her notebook,
dove deep into the stream of her dreams,
and soon, the world around her fell quiet.

PARALLEL

The textbooks in middle school made
Virginia feel like she wasn't there.
Her history reduced to a footnote to
America's story. She did independent study.
Read a Frederick Douglass biography.
Embraced lessons learned at her father's knee.

Parallel tracks. Existing side by side.
As a grown-up, Virginia would talk about
"parallel cultures." Would refuse the words:
majority, *minority*, because she was raised
knowing her history. Never minor or
less than, but equal. Parallel.

MEMORY

The stone steps into Glen Helen Gorge
once seemed built for giants.
At fifteen, she raced down them,
confident and sure.

This place brought back memories.
Layered history like the sandy
dolomite and shale cliffs
along the trail.

Memories that sparkled bright
in her mind's eye. Virginia would keep
this place inside herself—
always.

AWAY

Virginia walked beneath
tall towers. Shadows
cast on city concrete.
She held her head high.
Now twenty-four years old,
she'd moved away from
farms and family for
life in a different key.

A shy country import
to a crowded, busy place
swinging with jazz and
quick, sharp words. Inside,
Virginia carried words
and music from home.

Soon she met artists,
musicians, and poets.
A community of creative strivers.
Away from home, she would
make a new home in
New York City.

DOORS

It was difficult at first. When she knocked on the doors of opportunity, there was no answer. So, Virginia worked harder. Wrote more. Studied her favorite writers' perfect sentences. It was a time of uncertainty.

FAULKNER

WRIGHT

STEIN

JAMES

Then one door opened. She fell in love with a poet from the Bronx named Arnold. Different backgrounds but similar dreams. They wanted civil rights. To unite Black and white. They believed that their words could be part of that change.

Next came a writing opportunity. A friend had an idea. Perhaps one of the stories that Virginia had written at college would make a good children's book.

Virginia turned her short story, "The West Field," into her first book, *Zeely*. It was about a girl with a big imagination. About country places like Virginia's hometown. About country people, like Virginia's family.

HOME

Virginia, Arnold, and their kids moved back to her hometown. They built a new house on family land. Mother lived across the field. Cousins just down the road. The hogs and chickens were gone, but the place still felt familiar and inspired stories. Home.

Virginia was a star of the writing world. Flying higher than she'd ever imagined. In 1975, she won the Newbery Medal for her novel *M.C. Higgins, the Great*. In this book, a teenage boy worries about his future and family. About the safety of their home.

Virginia traveled across the US and around the world. But her most extravagant trips were in her mind. Extraordinary magic born from dreams. Stories about young people struggling to understand their place in a complicated world. And, like Virginia, they always find their way home.

AUTHOR'S NOTE

Virginia Hamilton believed that words and stories have the power to inspire a brighter future. She wrote more than forty children's books in many genres: realistic fiction, mystery, folktale, biography, and fantasy. She was the first Black woman to win the Newbery Medal and the Hans Christian Andersen Award. In addition, she received a MacArthur Fellowship "Genius Grant" and won the National Book Award, multiple Coretta Scott King Book Awards, the Boston Globe–Horn Book Award, and numerous others.

Hamilton's stories centered Black children at a time when there were very few children's books written with them in mind. She created relatable stories and characters, often adding a magical supernatural touch that stretched just beyond the possible into the world of dreams. She believed that books could be revolutionary, social justice tools, calling some of her works "liberation literature" (*The People Could Fly, Many Thousand Gone, Anthony Burns . . .*).

Hamilton felt strongly that children deserved books about things that mattered to them, and her characters give voice to big feelings. Some express fierce sibling or cousin rivalry. Others struggle with mentally ill family members or homelessness. Some face dangers that seem too big for them to handle. She approached these situations with great empathy and understanding.

Her concept of "parallel culture" reflects her experience growing up in a small, close-knit Black community in a quiet corner of southwestern Ohio. Family was three generations of the Perry clan—her mother's people. They farmed land on the edge of town, growing most of what they ate, though not enough to earn all they needed. Virginia's father worked in town at Antioch College as the dining room head waiter for over thirty years, and her mother worked as a housekeeper and sold extra produce from the farm. Books and ideas were important to family life and so was music. Her father was a talented mandolin player and Virginia sang beautifully. That legacy lives on—her son, Jaime, was a musician and is a children's book author; her daughter, Leigh, trained as a professional opera singer.

Each poem in this book is anchored by a single word and highlights anecdotes and themes that Hamilton shared in speeches, essays, and interviews. She believed that childhood could provide all that a writer needed to create fiction. With that in mind, I let her descriptions of people, places, and events from her younger years lead me to this re-creation of her past. Her novels provided insights as well, for even though they are not autobiographical, her childhood finds its way into many of her stories.

This book is for those who are curious about a creative life. My hope is that it will be read before or after *M.C. Higgins, the Great*; *Cousins*; *The House of Dies Drear*, or another of Virginia Hamilton's books. That her story will inspire young writers to fill notebooks with stories and poems. To create extraordinary magic.

TIMELINE

Early 1860s: Levi Perry is brought to Ohio by his mother.

1934: Virginia Esther Hamilton is born on March 12 in Yellow Springs, Ohio, to Etta Belle Perry Hamilton and Kenneth James Hamilton.

1938: Aunt Leah alerts the family about invaders from Mars after listening to H. G. Wells's *War of the Worlds* broadcast.

Baby photo of Virginia

1943: Virginia meets the Faceless One in her dreams and begins "The Notebook."

1947: Begins "The Novel." Reads Shirley Graham's *There Once Was a Slave*, a biography of Frederick Douglass.

1952: Graduates Bryan High School in Yellow Springs at the top of her class. Enrolls in Antioch College on full scholarship.

1956: Transfers to Ohio State University in Columbus, Ohio. Majors in literature and creative writing.

1958: Graduates Ohio State University. Moves to New York City. Studies fiction writing at the New School for Social Research. Meets Arnold Adoff, a white, Jewish poet, at a Charles Mingus jazz performance at the Five Spot nightclub.

1960: Marries Arnold Adoff.

1963: Daughter, Leigh, is born.

1967: Son, Jaime, is born. Her first book, *Zeely,* is published. *Zeely* is named an ALA Notable Book and wins the Nancy Bloch Award.

1968: *House of Dies Drear* wins the Edgar Allan Poe Award. Arnold Adoff publishes *I Am the Darker Brother: An Anthology of Modern Poems by Negro Americans.*

1969: Virginia and her family move to Yellow Springs, Ohio, and build their dream home on family land.

1971: *Planet of Junior Brown* wins a Newbery Honor Book award and the Lewis Carroll Shelf Award.

1974: *M.C. Higgins, the Great* wins the Newbery Medal, the National Book Award, the Boston Globe–Horn Book Award, and other honors.

1979: Is a delegate to the Second International Conference of Writers for Children and Youth in Moscow.

1982: *Sweet Whispers, Brother Rush* wins the Coretta Scott King Award, the Boston Globe–Horn Book Award, a Newbery Honor Book award, and other honors.

1984: Kent State University hosts the Virginia Hamilton Lecture in Children's Literature. This becomes the Virginia Hamilton Conference on Multicultural Literature for Youth.

1985: *The People Could Fly* wins the Coretta Scott King Award and other honors.

1987: Virginia and Arnold are named distinguished visiting professors at Queens College in New York.

1988: *In the Beginning: Creation Stories from Around the World* receives a Newbery Honor Book award, an ALA Best Book for Young Adults, and other honors.

1990: Awarded the Regina Medal of the Catholic Library Association.

Virginia with her cousin Marlene

1992: Awarded the Hans Christian Andersen Award for her body of work. Diagnosed with breast cancer.

1993: Travels to Japan for the Pacific Rim Conference in Kyoto.

1995: Receives the MacArthur Fellowship and the Laura Ingalls Wilder Award.

2002: Dies on February 19, 2002, at the age of sixty-seven.

2010: The Coretta Scott King–Virginia Hamilton Award for Lifetime Achievement is presented for the first time to Walter Dean Myers.

A SELECTED LIST OF VIRGINIA HAMILTON BOOKS

Zeely, illustrated by Symeon Shimin, 1967

The House of Dies Drear, illustrated by Eros Keith, 1968

The Time-Ago Tales of Jahdu, illustrated by Nonny Hogrogian, 1969

The Planet of Junior Brown, 1971

W. E. B. Du Bois: A Biography, 1972

M.C. Higgins, the Great, 1974

Paul Robeson: The Life and Times of a Free Black Man, 1974

Arilla Sun Down, 1976

Justice and Her Brothers, 1978. The first book of the Justice Trilogy

Dustland, 1980. The second book of the Justice Trilogy

The Gathering, 1981. The third book of the Justice Trilogy

Sweet Whispers, Brother Rush, 1982

Willie Bea and the Time the Martians Landed, 1983

The People Could Fly: American Black Folktales, illustrated by Leo and Diane Dillon, 1985

Anthony Burns: The Defeat and Triumph of a Fugitive Slave, 1988

In the Beginning: Creation Stories from Around the World, illustrated by Barry Moser, 1988

The All Jahdu Storybook, illustrated by Barry Moser, 1991

Drylongso, illustrated by Jerry Pinkney, 1992

Many Thousand Gone: African Americans from Slavery to Freedom, illustrated by Leo and Diane Dillon, 1993

Her Stories: African American Folktales, Fairy Tales, and True Tales, illustrated by Leo and Diane Dillon, 1995

Jaguarundi, illustrated by Floyd Cooper, 1995

Bluish: A Novel, 1999

The Girl Who Spun Gold, illustrated by Leo and Diane Dillon, 2000

Bruh Rabbit and the Tar Baby Girl, illustrated by James Ransome, 2003

A comprehensive list of Virginia Hamilton's books can be found at virginiahamilton.com/virginia-hamilton-books/

Virginia, Jaime, Leigh, and Arnold in 1982

A SELECTED BIBLIOGRAPHY

Adoff, Arnold, and Kacy Cook, eds. *Virginia Hamilton: Speeches, Essays, and Conversations.* New York: Blue Sky Press, 2010.

Mikkelsen, Nina. *Virginia Hamilton.* New York: Twayne Publishers, 1994.

Rubini, Julie K. *Virginia Hamilton: America's Storyteller.* Athens, OH: Ohio University Press, 2017.

More about Virginia Hamilton can be found at virginiahamilton.com.

Additional research sources: Library of Congress—Virginia Hamilton Papers, the Antioch College Archives, and Greene County Community Library.

Notes on the sources for each poem can be found at ninacrews.com/em-booknotes.